Introduction

Sometimes you will see people that catch your attention because they look different than anyone you have ever seen. They could be wearing something you are unfamiliar with, have unique markings, or be doing something you've never seen anyone do before. Everyone is unique and deserves to be treated with respect. When you see someone that you are curious about, it is best to be kind and polite.

Shaping Helmet

Sometimes you may see a child with a helmet that isn't used for riding a bike or playing sports. The child in the illustration is wearing a special kind of helmet that helps to shape his head. These children were born with a head shaped differently than most children. Sometimes a child is born with a flat spot or an oval-shaped head. The helmet they wear helps their head grow into a rounder shape.

[Model: Declan Pizzano Hurley]

Feeding Tubes

A feeding tube is used by people who have trouble eating. Sometimes they have a hard time eating because they are sick, don't have the use of their mouth or throat, or are recovering from surgery. Doctors will insert the feeding tube through the skin on the patient's belly and into the stomach. They use the feeding tube by adding a smooth mixture of food into the device that flows through the tube and into the stomach to nourish their body.

When they no longer need the feeding tube, the doctor will remove it and the patient can start to eat by chewing and swallowing their food again.

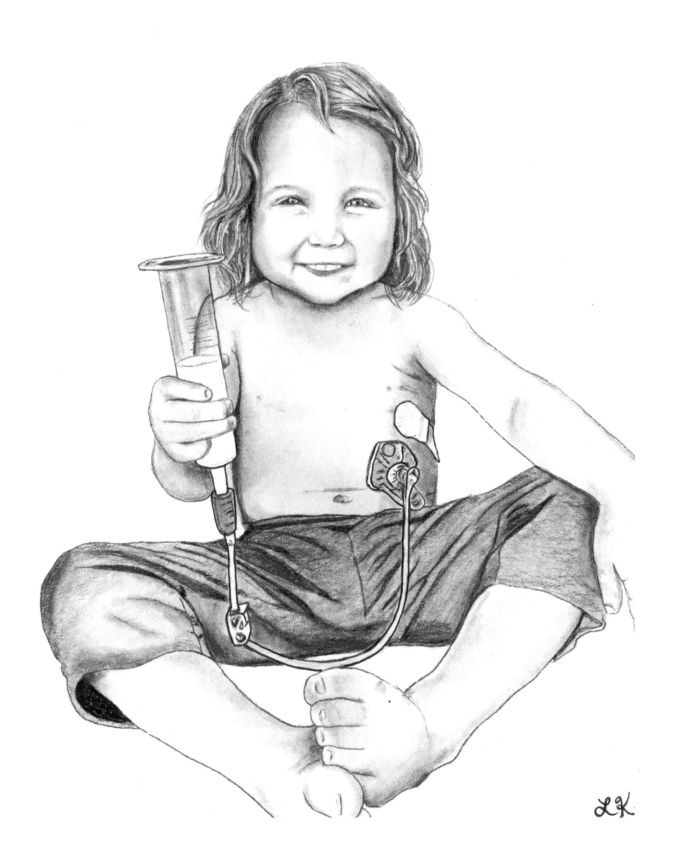

[Model: Riley Paige Sullivan]

Tattoos, Piercings, and Hair Dye

Sometimes you will see a person with tattoos, piercings, and dyed hair. Tattoos are only for adults because a needle is used to put ink into the skin. This changes the color of the skin permanently. Piercings can be small or very large and almost anywhere on a person's body. Hair dye is used to change the color of a person's hair. This man's beard is dyed pink, purple, and blue. He also has tattoos on his cheeks, forehead, and eye lids, along with piercings on his nose, cheeks, and lips. People sometimes change their appearance as an artistic way to express themselves. Some artists put their art on canvas, paper, stone or wood. Some people put art on their bodies so they can always carry it with them. All art is beautiful and deserves respect.

[Model: Spooky Graves]

Hijab

The woman in this illustration describes herself as a Muslim, which means she follows the religion of Islam. She wears a hijab, which is a head wrap that covers her hair, shoulders, and neck. Everyone has different reasons for choosing what they wear. It is important not to label or exclude anyone because of their appearance. It is best to be respectful and kind towards people regardless of their clothing or how they express themselves.

[Model: Yasmin Alsaleh]

Breastfeeding

Breastfeeding is the way a mother feeds her baby or young child with milk directly from her breast. Sometimes you will see a mother feeding her child this way. It is best to be respectful to the child and try not to disturb them while they are feeding. A child may get hungry or thirsty at any time and may need to have milk while they are away from home. It isn't always comfortable for the mother to breastfeed in public, so please be kind and use a gentle voice when you are near them.

Did you know? – Humans are mammals. The word "mammal" comes from the Latin word "mamma" which means "breast".

[Models - Jennifer Evans and Anna Evans]
[Photographer of reference photo: Brooklyn Rae Logan]

Hearing Aids

Most hearing aids are devices that make sounds louder for people who are deaf or hard-of-hearing. That is the type of hearing aid the boy on the next page is using. The illustration below shows a cochlear implant, which is a unique type of hearing aid. Instead of making sounds louder, a cochlear implant gives the person a kind of hearing that is unlike the way most people hear. Doctors implant part of the device into a person's head near their ear. This connects to a microphone outside the head. The microphone gives a signal to the implant. The implant does the work that the cochlea, or inner ear, would normally do, allowing the person to hear.

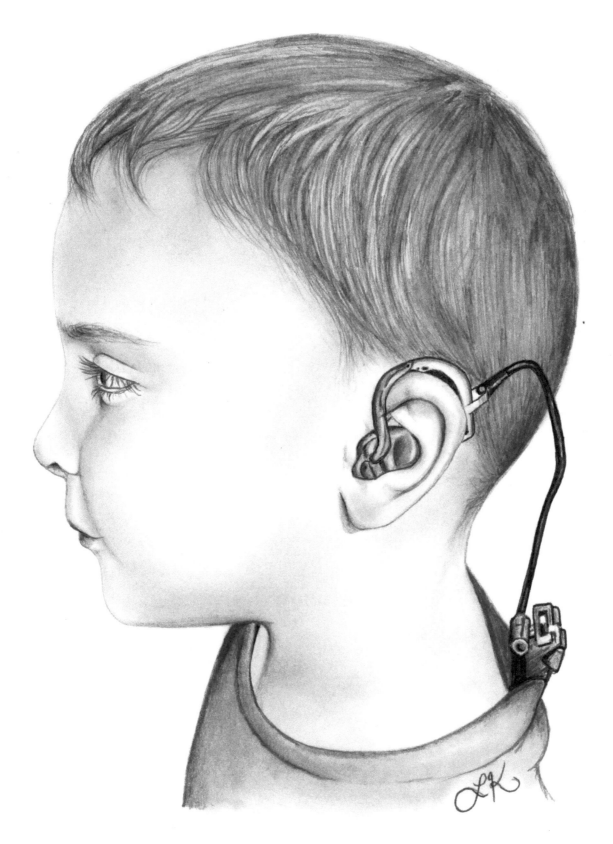

[Model: Joe Gioe Gregoire]

Limb Reduction and Amputees

Sometimes you will see a person who has one hand rather than two. The woman in this illustration was born with one hand. "Limb Reduction" is the term a doctor would use to describe a person's condition who was born with a shorter or missing arm or leg. An amputee is a person that has had a limb removed or reduced.

Some people who have unique physical characteristics are accustomed to getting curious looks and questions. However, it is rude to stare or to ask impolite questions. Try becoming friends with the person first and when they are ready, they may tell you their story.

[Model – Annie Garofalo]

Wheelchairs

Wheelchairs are used by people that have difficulties walking or cannot walk due to illness, injury, or disability. Wheelchairs come in many different styles. Sometimes they are manual which means that the person using the wheel chair will use their hands to push the wheels and move the chair. There are also handles on the back of a manual chair so another person can push the wheelchair from behind. An electric wheel chair, like the one in the illustration, is controlled with a joy stick and uses electric motors to move the chair.

[Model: June Lustenberger]

Drag Queen

Sometimes you will see a man that wears clothing, make up, and hair styles that women usually wear. The man in this illustration describes himself as a "drag queen, husband, father, friend, brother and son." He is wearing a gold sequined dress with feathers, glitter, and a large blonde wig. He wears these when he is performing in shows. His work is important to him because he brings people together, helps people with their emotions, and raises money for charities and benefits.

Did you know? – The word "Drag" derives from the phrase "Dressed As Girl" from Shakespearean times, when all performers had to be men.

[Model: Brian Kovalski]

Bindi and Sari

Sometimes you will see a woman that wears a bindi [bin-dee] on her forehead between her eyes. Bindis are worn for many reasons. Some women wear them to show that they are married, while others wear them simply as an accessory (like jewelry). It is traditionally worn by women of Indian decent that practice the Hindu religion.

The woman in this illustration is wearing a bindi and a sari [sah-ree]. A sari is a decorative piece of cloth that is worn around the waist and draped over the shoulders. She says, "Wearing traditional clothing like this makes me feel strong and makes me feel connected to my culture and my family."

Did you know? – The sari is a symbol of grace in the cultures of the Indian subcontinent.

[Model: Madhuri Patel]

Twins

Sometimes you will meet twins. Twins are siblings that were born together. Identical twins often look so similar to one another that you may not be able to tell them apart. Fraternal twins do not necessarily look the same and can even be different genders. You may also see triplets or quadruplets-three or four siblings who were born together!

Did you know? – Identical twins do not have identical fingerprints.

[Models: Mark and John Carney]

[Models: Kyran and Ryan Jolicoer]

Eye Patch

Sometimes you will see a person wearing a patch over one eye. It may be a cloth patch attached around the head by an elastic band or a string, an adhesive bandage, or a patch clipped to a pair of glasses. It is often worn by people to cover a lost or injured eye. It can also be used as a treatment for amblyopia [am-blee-oh-pee-uh], also known as lazy eye. The eye patch forces the amblyopic eye to strengthen by patching the good eye.

Did you know? - Amblyopia is the most common cause of visual impairment among children, affecting approximately 2 to 3 out of every 100 children.

[Model: Lilyanna]

Service Dogs

A service dog is a type of assistance dog specifically trained to help people who have a disability. The disability could be visual impairment, hearing impairments, mental illness, seizures, mobility impairment, diabetes, or many other conditions. When a service dog is working, it will usually wear a vest so you can tell it is service dog. It is very important not to touch or play with them unless the dog's owner invites you to.

Did you know? – Some service dogs help people with disabilities that you cannot see. For example, a person who is afraid to be in a store may have a service dog that helps them feel calm while they are shopping.

[Model: Dexter]

[Model: Sarah Ann Woodcock and Brody]

Love

People can love other people regardless of their gender, color, religion, etc. You can tell that two people love each other by the way they act with one another. Sometimes they will hold hands, kiss, or hug each other. Sometimes they will live together or become parents together.

Two women can fall in love with each other
or
a man and woman can fall in love with each other
or
two men can fall in love with each other
or
a dark skinned man and a light skinned woman can fall in love with each other

and so on...

People of any gender, race, ability, religion, culture, clothing style, etc. can fall in love with each other, become friends with one another, or be family members.

[Models: Pascal and Serge]
[Photographer of reference photo: Nicole Tozier]

African Head Wrap

The head wrap usually completely covers the hair and is held in place by tying the ends into knots close to the head. There are several ways to wear a head wrap. Some can be intricate and colorful and some can be simple and plain. Both men and women can be seen wearing a head wrap. There are many reasons people wear them including fashion, modesty, and religious beliefs.

[Model: Natalie Taylor]

Birthmarks

There are several different kinds of birthmarks. They can be large or small, raised or smooth, and almost any shape. They can be many different colors, however they are typically red, pink, purple, or brown. Birthmarks are not painful or itchy and they are not contagious.

The child in the illustration has a small, round, raised birthmark on his forehead and a large, smooth, multicolored birthmark on his cheek.

Did you know? - Birthmarks can either appear at birth or form after birth. Some can even fade as the child grows up.

[Model: Anonymous]

Child with Glasses

Sometimes you will see a child wearing eyeglasses. Glasses have a frame that holds two lenses and rests on the nose and behind the ears. Someone with poor vision looks through the lenses and is able to see more clearly. It is more likely that you will see adults wearing glasses, but occasionally a child will also need them. It can be difficult for a child to adjust to wearing glasses so it is best to be gentle and kind to them. You can say that you like their glasses and that will make them feel happy. Giving a compliment is a great way to make a friend.

[Model: Joseph Alan McAndrew]

These are just a few of the unique people you may see. Be a leader in showing kindness. If others see you being kind, they will follow and more will follow them. You never run out of love, so give a lot and give it often.

Author's Note: I hope this book can be a lesson in tolerance for all ages. While interviewing the models in this book, I was told many startling stories of how impolite some people can be when approaching a unique person. It is my goal to get to the core of the problem. We can teach our children at home to go out into the world with a kind and open heart. We can help them understand what they are seeing without being rude.

About the writing: Exposure to big words and bigger concepts is good for children – especially if it comes from someone they look up to. This book is designed to enlighten children and adults alike. A child and an adult being on the same learning plane can be an excellent way to bond and grow together. Show your child that learning never ceases and tolerance for all people is an honorable quality.

About the content: I did my best to be as politically correct and factual as possible. Some words and phrases used in this book will work for some people and may not for others.

About me: Hi! I'm Lisa. I grew up in Methuen, MA and live in New Hampshire now. I'm a mother and wife. I'm an artist, a teacher, and a community leader. I work hard. I get sad sometimes and I get happy sometimes. I love adventures. I worry about the world. I rock out in my kitchen and sing my heart out in the car. That's who I am. I overthink...I make mistakes...I'm silly...I'm powerful...I'm weak...and I love.

Acknowledgements

Editors:

AJ Koehler

Marisa Delhay

Special Thanks:

Michelle Harding

Shannon Rene Scott

Thomas Perry

Dedicated to:

My family, friends, and community.

Thank you all for your endless support and love. I would not have been able to do this without you!